A Line or

Robert Drake

Robert L. Drake

BaD Writers' Press

First published in May 1991 by

BaD Writers' Press
c/o Artworks
Barrow Borough Council
Piel View House
Abbey Road
Barrow-in-Furness
Cumbria LA13 9BD

ISBN 0 9517581 0 1

Typeset by **Chris and Candy Chuter**

Printed and Bound by:

PRINT iT (NOTTM) LTD
Unit 2. Elizabeth Court
Manners Ind. Est
Ilkeston
Derbyshire
Tel: (0602) 442063

The financial assistance of Northern Arts and Artworks (Barrow Borough Council) is gratefully acknowledged.

For

my Mum and Dad

Contents

Acknowledgements

Some of these poems first appeared in the following:

BaD Writing; Envoi; Iron; Local Arts UK; the North West Evening Mail; Orbis; Poems 90 (Lancaster Literature Festival); Poetry Cumbria 5; Poetry Wales; Vision On (Ver Poets); and have been broadcast on 'Write Now', BBC Network Northwest.

Inscriptions was commissioned by the 1990 National Garden Festival at Gateshead as part of their *Texts in the Landscape* project, with financial support from Northern Arts. The piece was carved on stone by Bryant Fedden.

Builders

I

With bricks and blocks sheer walls are built, tight-coursed
on constant beds of mortar, hung from stringlines
held taut against the curved earth's pull. Exact
dimensions govern skill; mistakes soon grow
malignant, cancering the concrete skin.
Spot-board and trowel, lump-hammer, bolster, level,
a good eye, and raw finger-ends; the syntax
of brickwork spills from under the segged thumbs
of men delighting in the long run, doorways
and window-gaps their only punctuation.
Unhindered, brickies would enfold the world
with their bank verse; unbroken cliffs of grey
and red and yellow, solid barricades
to shut out space from habitation's page.

II

I build with stones: crude quarried blocks;
      smooth beck-tumbled cobbles; ice-worn, frost-cracked
      foreigners; old seabeds.
Mocking arithmetic, their random shapes
dictate place and purpose: throughs, wall-wide;
      cams for the top; quoins for each wall-head.
Stone walls scrawl across a half-written manuscript,
outlining jewel-bright fields, funnelling beasts
from open fell to byre or in-by land.

A good eye's useful, but the blind
could wall; I turn and turn each stone
to find its face by touch, turn it again
to rhyme cusp with hollow, snagging
the hard lug of a dead sea-creature
between frozen ridges of ancient sand.
The eye may see, but it is the hand
that judges, adjusts, aligns, then lingers,
caressing firm flanks of naked wall.

The work is shot through with holes.
Weasels and wagtails delight in crannies;
the waller's pride is in well-crafted
interstices of stone: smoots and squeeze-stiles;
      Stepping-stiles and lunkeys;
      hogg-holes and cripples.
Sheep jostle in the low doorways.
Tags of wool caught on rough stones
flutter as the wind finds space to slip through.

III

As a dam-burst of tumbled wall is gathered
among tussocks and gullies
I reap the broad stonefield of words.

How quickly scattered rubble wastes
into impoverished soil!
Some stone at least from every gap is lost.

As nightfall closes down the fell I carry home
a meagre crop balanced
precariously between my shoulders

meaning to build the salvaged images
into strong lines
before the barricades of sleep encircle me.

At midnight a cooling fire collapses
inwards on itself.
I rub at grit behind my eyelids

dream of burst-open walls tumbling
downhill, wake startled
by the crash of falling scaffolding.

Walls

As though a net had been cast,
had snagged on high ground,
ripped in places by sharp ridges,
had settled into each hollow
and turned to stone;

as though the fells must be held down,
weighted against equinoctial gales,
dressed up in lace of lichen,
waiting for a farmer's slack time;
as though they have nothing better to do,

walls fall across my path,
marking my days with their calm stone tread.
I haul myself along them, rest in their shelter,
take home their dust under my fingernails,
sleep exhausted, dreaming of them:

still the only glyph on earth's crust
visible from space.

Stones

They are all there, waiting; weathered faces
scarred by downfall, bones gleaming in the bright
suddenness of day. Before the cool night
I will have put them back in their places
and the long bandage of time and darkness.

It helps to know how they were used before,
though this arrangement is my own; the core
rubble-filled as always, but the fitness
of shapes neighbouring along rough courses
as distinctive as language. The grammar
of stones exercises hand and hammer
while the mind breaks apart clogged words, forces
tired images to work along new seams,
resists the collocation of lexemes.

Setting to Work

The first job; to sort among the stone - throughs,
cams, footings, wallers, fill - displayed on grass
like lexical analysis. Then, choose;
not as words are blindly plucked from the mass
of language, but rather as poets pick
exact phrases to flense spirit from flesh:
the waller parses sentences of rock.

Sometimes there is abundance, and then, flush
with stone, walls babble extravagantly
about fellsides. More often there is dearth,
economies of rubble, constantly
revising, adjusting, reducing girth,
and striking out whole paragraphs of stone
to ensure what remains stands on its own.

Riving Slate

I'll open a fresh page of stone: you'll see.

In the tin shed, drummed by insistent rain,
one slate clog rests against my padded knee.
On its sawn edge I gauge an unseen line,
sketch with steel the white rune of opening -
magic performed countless times before night,
but not diminshed for all that. The ring
of steel on metal deepens, driving light
where even light has forgotten itself.

The foreman makes notes, passers-by peer in:
he tallies finished slates, they watch the half-
opened piece riven, riven cardboard-thin.
Murmur at skill they may: to them each clean
stone face's expression remains unseen.

Opening

The chisel marks a line on stone
as though light showed round a closed door,
seen from a dark room. My hammer nails the chisel
confidently: unlocked, the door opens.

Amongst stones I work easily.
This one is too deep: I must dock
the back side until it sits snug,
face lined up with the other faces.

This stone is too thick: I must rive
a page or two from it, pare it down
to the size of neighbours, form
a level bed for the next course.

My chisel marks a way into the stone.
Unlocked, the door opens: light
trembles, remembering itself in stone-dust.
Split crystals smile out ambiguously.

Erratic

Now, having come so far
(that glacier's hard belly!)
striations, these travel lines,
are wearied by millenniums
of lichen.

Rootless and strange,
run aground, tied down
by impertinent fibres - tree
sinews are stronger, briefly,
than stone.

It is time to move on:
the ice age is long
overdue.

Altar

Praying, he'd lay his forehead in this cool hollow:
see the faint smudge, a shortened lifetime's sweat?

On this scorched top blood seethed under sacrifices:
their heat accepted here, provoking jealousy.

Soft steps. A cry, choked off. Fresh blood, fly-
blackened. In the hurt silence cold words formed:

What have you done? The voice of your brother's
blood cries to me from this stone.

Doorstep

I was placed here in 1878.
The first occupants to come through the gate
(man, wife, four children - aspiring gentry)
stepped on me daily but never saw me.

They, and their successors, wore me away;
he going out to work, the children to play.
She merely spoke; I was, by her command,
scrubbed by a daily with thick red hands.

Messages passed on, farewells and greetings,
I witness all, departures and meetings;
preserve comings and goings through this door
daily - but not, perhaps, for evermore.

In the mid-1960s I was turned
over, the pride of my cupped welcome scorned
in favour of flat, blank modernity -
daily milk-bottles need stability.

My latest owner just cannot decide
whether to turn me, restoring my pride,
or leave me inverted, bolstering his
as I bow for his daily passages.

Fell Walls

The hot river steams up a lens
of cold valley air. Beneath
the morning mask a people drone
about their lives. The mist clears
and recurs; day and night flicker
across our faces like cloud-shadows
on the everlasting moor we define,
clouds and shadows on the fells
whose broken bones we are,
whose bony fingers we restrain.

Not much made or growing matches
our endurance. The good mason's work
survives in the village; oaks
share in our patient observation
of transience. They have a nearer
viewpoint, and the dangers
that confers. Rarely are we taken,
but hear the whine of saws, see
raw brown tears flow down
pasture across the valley.

Up here little beyond ourselves
occurs. The tic of a farmer's grief
or passion; the morning of a generation;
the afternoon and evening of a dynasty:
these are the light and shade
of our long day. But while we stand
above all, watchful, brant fields
slip and crack, betray our roots:
we slide, slow cold rivers water-
falling into the hurrying valley.

Pebble in a City Park

In the beginning: light. A thousand suns
glare into this compact palimpsest of darkness,

half-waking memories. In creation's fire
all atoms shiver; earth becomes formless, void.

The god drones steadily away, a silver point
in the blue above its worst imaginings.

Amid desolation the first beings stir;
small thick-skinned crawling creatures, already

mutating inside their shells. The upright ones
come next: some, helmeted, survive;

some, eye-sockets weeping grotesque tears, fade
like the rain-storms among encircling hills.

And nearby here, a wall that bears the shadow
of a standing figure, head tilted back.

All round that outline scorched, rewritten
stone loses its memory of an unuttered scream.

Gray Croft Stone Circle

Much has changed: some things are changeless. Westward, the broad pasture, sea, strives incessantly to erode earth between us; eastward, the firm features of mountains are relentlessly dissolved. To the south, above the shoulder of bent grasses, gulls wheel ceaselessly; northward, the perpetual lights, a vast city. We have fallen, and risen like the tides of generations stored in our permanent darkness, their clamour crystallised in hard silence. But in these last days, into our changeless watchfulness come shrieks and dribbles of degeneration, strings of light weaving a cold web
of cor uption through our stone heart
dis l ving the stern pag of memor ,
eras g the ecor that will ing ev
o justic h l st re s len
na
d a
ri
e
n
. O

Keystone

The hands that eased me into place
made me a cold red Samson, endlessly
shouldering aside twin curved downfallings of stone.

Many hands have held me - dragged
naked from the quarried block,
appraised by the knowing touch of calloused fingers,

dressed fitly for this task,
a fine ribbed border setting off
the scalloped features of my broad wedged face.

It was the trains that blinded me

(their million battering passages,
a century's soot clogging my pores)
until... a change occurred, a deeper note felt.

Now cold hands of rain rinse grime
from my long blindness. The white trains,
their canisters gleam in the sun. Against my shoulders

arch-stones shiver: foundations tremble.

Notes on Stone

Stone. It does not breed.
No fertile cells spawn;
spring leaves it cold.

Lungless, it draws no breath;
without mind, thinks nothing.
Stone has a heart (masons break it)
but cannot feel, immured by tough skin.

Limbless, stone's crystal skeleton
endlessly resonates; frequencies
marking time, beating on walls
of ancient imprisoned light.

Tongueless, stone mouths no words.
Still, earth's black box waits to be
unlocked, replayed.

Wall Gap

Today, this is my work:
to scrabble through a white ruck
of stone, tumbled where the wall grew slack
as foundations shifted on sloping bedrock;
to find three misplaced stones and set them back
more firmly; meanwhile trying not to think
too much of how this labour is like
us, searching for the hidden crack
within our marriage. But, mend or break,
we've set ourselves the task.

Today this bitch
wall takes a rough touch;
one big footing to turn over with a lurch
of muscles, then a search to locate such
stones as will sit on this awkward arch
of rock. Dinner-time comes with not much
to show, and the spare hour hatches
ferreting thoughts that chafe and itch,
that drive me back before time to patch
the break my hands can reach:

whereas tonight, left
alone with each other, faced with a rift
fingers are powerless to draw shut,
sitting together in silence that is at best
free from recrimination, I will recall the last
hour's work; out of stone, exhausted
by searching, and carrying gifts
and scraps from other wall-gaps, thinking that
the left-overs of another time may not
be enough to replace what has been lost.

Poem for Sarah

You paused for a moment in the kitchen doorway
and your ten-year-old turmoil and awkwardness
fell away. I saw the women in you, smiling back at me
easily, face and limbs in their lean fullness.

And more than this: I saw our troubles
having end and purpose, being the bricks we pile
together to make the distinctive *us* -
an adolescence of tears may be worth one smile

like yours this morning. An aching tenor
with a sad piano played on the radio, fortuitously.
Caught for an instant motionless between desire
and regret, tears prickled my eyelids insistently,

and through their lens the moment was photographed.
The song faded. Somewhere a voice called out.
The kindly earth began to turn again, spinning
you towards your womanhood; me towards... what?

Ferment

Going to the kitchen late that night
I froze, reaching out for the light-switch,
stopped by a sharp new sound, by urgent
wine-time ticking through the airlock's curves.
Light then showed that sullen yellow must
had woken, caddis-larvae of yeast
tumbling and soaring, rising bubbles
exploding in the glass jar's narrows.

Mocked by the unwelcome counterpoint
of randy yeast to my discontent
I stood as through stripped naked: heard fresh
tobacco hiss in my cigarette,
felt the ferment bubbling through my veins,
froth of desire gathering in my groin.

Turk's Head Lilies

Some time in the early morning the sun
must have woken these, splitting open strange
fruits and peeling back their skins to display
crude inner lips, hideously orange

fading to yellow, darkly blotched. What's worse,
each flower's lewd nakedness protrudes; six
slender stems ending in what look like small
ham rolls... These circle, trembling, a male sex

organ, whose rampant purple tip waits
to be stroked. But what sinister, botched insect
could justly pleasure such ugly, wanton
blooms? Not the day, but the night (I suspect)

has spawned them; not the Creator, but
a jealous rival, working secretly, in poor
light. I wish I had not passed by here!
Forgive me, God, if after all they're your

making; criticism's easy, I know,
especially when time's short, the kids must
be met from school, the washing done, and just
one brief hour's writing most days will allow.

A Last Fling in the Woods

Beneath stark naked branches, under a crackling
bedspread of leaves, the fungal orgy's in full swing.

Pale-buttocked puffballs heave from the covers;
phallic stink-horns thrust probing hyphae

into soft yielding decay - necrophiliacs, all
of them, with the hard black ache of cramp balls,

or delicate grisettes of vaginal mould:
infected genitalia of the underwood.

Here, an erect nipple; there, a swollen clitoris,
indulge in the concupiscence of rottenness,

a promiscuous last supper, scenting cataclysm
in the wind of their bacchanalian autumn;

a last pungent fuck before the holocaust -
their armageddon, the bomb-flash of frost.

Heron

A gawky adolescent
crash-landing
great wings flapping
like an unbuttoned coat.
A black and white cap
on backwards
a striped school tie
down the impossible
jughandle throat.
An outrageous hen
stalking through marestail
suddenly   frozen
neck like a white arm
holding the dagger
poised to decide.

Sparrowhawk

After that long morning's vertical downpour
dinner-time brought out a sudden broom; a fresh gale
carded the atmosphere's fleece, and from torn

clouds plunged cataracts of brightness: light fell
in pulsing, shifting columns, streaming from where
rain so recently had fallen in an endless veil.

The gale growled to itself now in the high air,
swept through the coppice with a last slap of rain,
roaring at the beeches, caught in their knotty hair.

Sunk deep between calm walls the narrow lane
was my safe harbour, hollow and still, while
the wind tore itself free again and again.

And here she flickered past me, beautiful;
so close I could believe her talons scored my cheek.
A brief smudge of blown smoke, lemon and charcoal;

then arrow-fast, close-winged, all pivot and flick,
she faultlessly plunged through a heaving sea
of branches, deft as a conjuror's trick,

leaving the lane silenced by her deadly
intent: gone, quicker than drawn breath,
sooner than tongue could name her cruel beauty,

quicker than the missed heartbeat of a little death.

Silver

Tired of opening black earth wicked with root-stalks
I glanced across to Town Bank beyond jumbled grey roofs.
The pigeons turned in that instant, their breasts silvering
the hill, and (vanishing on the turn) hooked back again
to warm their upper wings in the bright afternoon.

They formed a silver pennant waving a joyous message;
a silver shuttle flickering across the loom of green,
weaving a glittering thread into the fabric of spring;
a carillon of silver bells to summon unburst buds:
begin that slow flight downwards to the patient earth.

Canvas

In afternoon sunlight the limed field gleamed
across the valley. Tractor-marks formed faint
brush-strokes of dusty green, and so it seemed
as though bare canvas showed through ragged paint
at the heart of a yet unfinished work,
between heavier textures, plantations
stippled with buds of purple birch, red oak,
and below flawless cobalt, air's ocean.

By morning a galleon fleet of clouds,
snagged on the high fells, let down their long lines
of drizzle, varnishing the hissing roads,
whitening stony becks and washing grains
of sweet lime into the black earth's gullet:
deft touches from a brilliant palette.

Flints

Tortured figures spill from torn ground,
white flesh sloughed off to the black bone.
    Knap them for weapons,
    split them for wall-stones,
    grip them with plum-roots,
    tie them with hop-vines,
    bury them under a carpet of wheat.
Hide them.   Only let sea's caress
polish them to pearls of dark glass.

Tap-roots

Summer's leftovers unpeel from empty soil;
a mulch of frost-withered leaves, unfruitful flowers,
and underneath, strewn grass on spring's flat news.
Papers suppress unwanted growth; hold down
moisture for roots to use. They rot slowly.

Yellowed but clear, the picture emerges;
a column of Chinese armour and one man dancing
in front of it. A river of steel and one man
damming it. Hours later blood flowed - his, maybe;
then tanks streamed through pitiful barricades.

Root-fibres have already taken hold
in old newsprint, halfway to humus, and the photograph
awakens memory's seeds that send down tap-roots
through Peking to Soweto, Londonderry to My Lai,
Amritsar to Wounded Knee, Glencoe to Bethlehem:

and deep into human darkness go filaments
from my belly; among Calleys, Krugers, Dyers,
Herods breaking children's skulls on stones;
seeking in history's deep loam nourishment for when
I'll stare into the round black mouth of death.

The Back Lane (for Kevin Fegan)

The back lane's as long as a cigarette.

Between a sycamored embankment and the twelve colours
of a dozen back gates, peopled on Thursdays
with black rubbish bags, the back lane waits.
By moonlight it is a stream to the streetlight river;
by starlight, a deep pool of shadows;
in fog, a tunnel under empty branches;
in summer, greened by new light through fresh leaves.

The back lane's a kind of lexicon.

Somewhere between the small drift of dead leaves
at the top end, and tangled brambles
behind a billboard at the street end;
somewhere between number 23 and the guest-house;
in the time of a smoke, a slow pace,
a glance up and down the main road;
in the time of a quickening return... words are found;

words are found. My chair creaks as I sit back in it.
The lamplight's pool settles; the page
clears of fog; words drift into place.
A diesel growls slowly along the embankment, and
under it the black lane, emptied, waits.

White Trains Log

MARCH. Woke
shaking from dreams
lay for a long time
while the train
grumbled away
through town.

APRIL. They
come hourly
through darkness
concealing
black suns radiant
on yellow skies.

JUNE. Night
too short and
threadbare now
to hide
the poisoned cups
they send.

SEPTEMBER. More
often than hours
the trembling
down deep
hugging myself
for comfort.

OCTOBER. Woke
to silence
five nights
and no trains
this, this
worst of all.

Restoring Gunpowder to its Former Use

Grandfathers might remember this place thrang
with folk and horses for the Hospital Parade;
some, perhaps, straws in their caps, waited for hiring
at the fairs of Martinmas and Whitsuntide.
That age passed. The town wears its old men like scars.
An age of dullness choked The Gill with cars.

But tonight, triumphantly, children and fire-
eaters blur and delete the white markings, and all
but the vehicles of our imaginations are
excluded by a ring of market stalls.
So hot-dog stands, street plays, laughter, noise,
restore this car-park to its former use.

The carnival is like all good Saturday nights
rolled together and tossed up into the dusk.
In a circle of expectant faces, a juggler waits
for nightfall, spinning three fires. *Isn't this,* asks
someone, shoulders jostling, neck craning to see,
Isn't this the way things ought to be?

A tale of masks, of crocodiles, of swans
threads through the weave and whirl of country dances,
until torchlight and a long calm chord quietens
all.   Fireworks flower in darkness; brilliance
of carnival exulting in our silence,
restoring gunpowder to its former use.

Lantern Parade

From evening's perfect folds of indigo
ghost pyramids and pale moons converge, frail
tissue chests on ribs of twisted willow.

Matches scrape at the signal, darkness: dull
paper lungs swell with a deep breath of gold.
The night, bare of moon that has fallen full

along our streets, peers over the shoulders
of watching houses, a grandstand of stars.
Between the Seven Sisters and the old

auction mart's spire bright and proximate Mars
learns of peace from our festival of light:
until at last we plunge, brief meteors,

welcomed into the extinguishing night.

Sarah Casey's Photograph

At Christmas one of us lodged a card
between the picture's glass and frame,
that covered half your face, all but
those eyes that pin me down,
their afterimage burning far beyond
the room. On the inverted tree
my Dad once drew (a medieval map
whose edges quickly blurred into
obscurity) you're root and trunk;
Whitehouse, then Casey; my unknown
Great Grandma.
                                        Look how your life
has rooted me, how Ireland aches
like a wound in my chest! See
how afraid I have become to speak
other than truth; pretensions wither
and evasions shrivel in the frost
of your unyielding stare.

This morning I removed the card:
I'll not suffer one moment more
the scalpel of your gaze untempered
by the small mercy of your smile.

Dad's War

The British Army helmet was enormous,
crowning seven slender years;
my turn to be an heroic mushroom,
my friend a Nazi, helmetlessly dead.
We hammered into their kitchen, firing
rat-a-tat sticks, and my Dad in ambush
snatched the helmet from my head -
...never want to see you wearing
one of these... I felt his hurt
and anger then for the first time,
though I was far from understanding.
My Dad's war clogs his throat.
Half a century gone since then,
and still he speaks in riddles
(*Gott mit uns* on a belt buckle?)
dark secrets of machine-guns
and strange place-names. He hobbles
round the house on ruined feet.

My youngest son, at seven, plays
with die-cast bombs; creates
a nuclear world, blows it apart
over and over in one afternoon.
I fight my own war in secret, without
my Dad's approval: *...they've kept*
the peace these forty years...
A kind of peace, maybe; a cauldron
of small wars not calling us
to helmets yet. I run my hand
across Tom's slender shoulders
hoping they'll bear that weight
the foolish generations place
on him and those still to be born:
hoping he'll see his own children
at seven playing games in summer
gardens where the alphabet
of war has been unlearned.

Chapel Island (The First Landing)

It is the gunnel of a sunken ship.
It is the remains of a hard knot
of time. All-comers from the open sea
have driven into each weak spot
and forced it apart. The rocks
fracture along their planes, split
and spring like neglected planks
on an old boat.
                    An ancient spirit
infects this place. Even the beach
pebbles waken; grey stones, black grit,
mutate into gull chicks that dart
into crevices, tremble and wait
for our shadows to pass. The adults
wheel, wheel in the wide bright
air, crying.
              Among ruins
foreign stone mingles with white
native limestone - like the faith
that came from deserts, brought
on winds, across seas, finding
little harbours, unbuilt-
on outcrops, hearts to break:

and both tears and sweat are salt.

Old Sailor

Turning, rough hand on my sleeve
in the white, rain-scoured lane, he searched
my eyes, the hedges, then far across the shining bay,
wincing his old face into gullies, capes and coves;
a strange shore I cannot visit.

Words, like blown bridges,
burnt and sunken ships, have foundered in the gulf
cleaving memory, tongue. All seas calm or crashing
well into his empty mouth, then fail on the dull spit
between his ocean and my stale lagoon.

Only a few drops splash
into the gullies; his eyes are wet sea-caves
I try to look out from, but see nothing, hearing
just the faint hiss of distant surf.

Alice

This drawer holds all I've left of him:
a photo - his arm round my waist,
a music-box with a dancing clown,
a painted egg in a glass case.

Sometimes at night I dream of him,
and really want to see him then.
I write him letters, but I've never
given them to my mum to send.

He used to take me to the zoo,
then we'd play trains at his old place.
We found a plane once, but it soon broke.
(A photo - his arm round my waist.)

I often ask my mum to drive
along the new street he lives down.
She won't - we go home another way.
(A music-box: a dancing clown.)

My auntie lives near him, and when
I stay I look out for his face,
until she calls me from the window.
(A painted egg in a glass case.)

Once we did see him, from the car.
He walked towards us - I smiled, waved,
but I don't think he recognised me.
The lights changed and we drove away.

This drawer holds a photograph -
a smudge of kisses on his face,
a clown that turns and turns and turns,
a broken egg in a glass case.

True

Too narrow this doorway to stretch out in, but
countless feet have worn the step to fit my bones

then pass all night through fitful sleep
long-legged giants - brogued, sandalled, high-heeled -

most thankfully oblivious, though a long stare
down from hooded eyes chills deeper than any stone.

I wait for early light staining pavements
oil and pearl, then rise to look for gold. It's true,

you see, the heavy coins drop without ring or burr
unnoticed by the giants, heads meshed in noise

so far above their feet that soon leave clear
streets gilded by the alchemy of dawn.

A New Jerusalem

Sighing, the sun clambers to the red rim
and treads deliberately, a tired old judge,
through a smudge of dust and woodsmoke
above the choking cardboard city, burning
on curves of corrugated iron.

A stock-exchange of shared standpipes, latrines;
strange commerce with cast-off fabric, cable,
waste metal; a spare unwanted people carve
their brief signature in baked earth, striving
to fence off the hungry mouth of death.

Goatherd children cross the steaming dump;
women cast round for a tin-can gleam, meaning food,
a cooking pot; under the mountain fathers dig
for tin, gold, diamonds. By evening
even their skins will seem like stone.

Nightfall. Among carefully averted eyes ride
soldiers, through silence. No one any longer tries
to pray for a weeping king who would, yes, ride
heeding unuttered sighs of grief and bitterness:
who would give back these stones their tongues.

The Breaking Wave

For an early hour in the station buffet
I watched dolphins burst from that small hill
of ocean heaved up by the hidden foot
of an awesome, outcurving cliff of steel
riding a continuous wave from port to port.
My train arrived; the dolphins I had to leave
frozen mid-leap in endless play.

A train and two hours later, eastward-bound
along the Tyne's continuously curving wave,
below Corbridge I saw cormorants on rocks
in midstream, hunched over the constant scroll
of fresh water, turning their backs
on the six bridges stitching Newcastle
to Gateshead through the river's wound:

and later still, perplexed by choice
(in the spare hours that railways give)
I felt the train curve through a junction
slick as the curl of a breaking wave.
Town-lights fled past like unasked-for advice
while in the cold black mirror indecision
carved beaked and winged shadows on my face.

Inscriptions

I

Tools mark stone with bright wounds,
    human pride with words:
time dulls the mason's scratches
    and frets at epitaphs.

II

As a thinning scalp
    stretches over bone
so the skin of our existence
    briefly fleshes stone.

III

In time there will be nothing
    but old light's freedom
from prisons of split crystals
    in stone's millennium.

Epitaphs

I'd hoped there might have been a sense
of triumph, approaching the stone last seen
freshly riven from its quarry, now sunk
on edge in grass, among immature trees.
Instead, imagined fanfares, silver balloons
in the bright air, punctured at the sight
of children sprawled across my work,
tracing inscriptions round the stone
until a shower rinsed them away like dust.

I thought then how an unseasonal frost
might have turned soft water to a fist of ice
striking flakes from sharp-edged lettering.

A fifty-year-long leap, and I am dead,
buried - gravestone-commemorated, perhaps.
Another half-century, and my departed
children have their own chiselled memorials.
Leap forward again, again and again, until
a time when other children run fingertips
across a moss-heavy stone, wondering
at faint marks, not quite decipherable...
once words: that now say everything.

Tom Faulkner

Fragments of a Novel

(October 1989 - August 1990)

Homecoming

After the car had gone
he touched the garden gate's cold latch;
remembered the exact hand-pressure needed
to free that tight sneck and not bruise
fingers on the iron bar beneath.

Under the overhanging birch...
through shoals of wind-blown alyssum seeds
along the path... left to itself the garden
clawed up to the cottage walls, windows
half-hidden by rampant virginia.

Taking in the cupped garden,
the cool dark shippon and the airy barn's
dustladen ladders of sunlight, he recognised
he'd lived there fifteen years
a blind fool not to see it all

a jewel brooched by trees.
Unshouldering his rucksack in the porch
shadowing its green dog-scrabbled door
(showing a century or more's petticoats
of paint) he found the key

that turned slick in the lock,
pushed open the door that grated over
a slate flag (as it had through all
his young days, seemingly wearing
neither wood nor stone)

and stepped into the kitchen
snuffing the sour must of disuse,
then moved from room to room, reclaiming
his childhood from their corners, touching
everything: touching and touching.

Summer

Darkening the kitchen doorway he smiled
down into her surprise at having him
home early. Her tea left half-drunk,
magazine forgotten open on the blue table;
impelled by urge he hauled her not unwilling
round the turn in high, wide oak stairs.

Below their window the nurseryman scratched
long rows, his hoe raising grey plumes of dust.
The red-faced twins dozed in their cage,
tiny diamonds of sweat above greedy mouths,
stubby fingers clutching at flannel,
kneading sleep's dream breast.

A few moments abandoning their clothes,
then themselves to the rut's rhythm,
shouting in time to the squeeze of juices:
    oh   oh   oh   oh   oh
    then   ah....

In the breath-catching afterwards,
blood's thunder receding, they heard
beneath the wide open window a hoe
resume its patient scrabbling.

The Big Wind

Tom...
To-om!
Her call a lone migrant warbler lost
in the storm. The bird of her call tumbled
down the big wind; the bubble of her call burst
around him. He heard. Not his name, but a fragment
of song in the storm's endless torment,
that turned his head to where she stood
by the door, hands holding her dress
down against the big wind's pressure.

Only their house still in the universe.

He crouched by freshly torn ground,
fingers stained with dandelion milk,
amazed by the green in the black, the seed
in the cracked rock, the worm in the wood:
appalled by his smallness under the big wind,
nameless and lost like a woodcock
hidden in dead leaves under the birch.

Nameless and lost. Still she stood in the porch,
and she waved. A small, hesitant motion,
but then enough to be his salvation.

A Small Paradise (Lost and Regained)

Go on... be off! You're no good to me
or yourself, when you're like this. I'll cope...
She smiled at his departing back
and the suddenly bright doorway.

Toecaps dug fierce holds in the slope.
Beyond the field's crest his little world
was hidden, forgotten in the immensity
of autumn light. The miner's track
drew him up through moist woodland,
ribs of naked stone among poor trees.

High on that fellside he found the rock,
a fallen slab of mountain incongruously
level in the clutter of a tilted stonefield;
sat on it for an hour while ravens
hunted carrion and the wounded sun
plunged to a distant but clear horizon.

At sunset, standing on the fell's shoulder,
he saw far below their small paradise
set in the brilliance of pasture;
a diamond of white and grey, paint and stone,
in a gold ring of briefly flaming trees.

Birds of Prey

The wind was full of splinters.
Ice pierced the falcon's eye; she glared
across the curve of crag, stirred,
stepped out on to the wind.

Hungry, she turned the valley
under her wings; the snaking ghyll,
the bracken-rusted slopes of fell -
nothing escaped her eye.

Her eyes: huge within their skull,
head turning them to focus on each kill.

A smudge dropped from the last pine
above the ruins of High Dixon Ground;
she watched the sparrowhawk's swiping bound,
marked their converging lines

of flight: hawk among woods,
falcon high on towers of humming air;
hawk through the edge of trees, and there
in a small clearing stood

a man, staring up, wide-eyed, mouth open -
hooked, man and hawk, in the eye of the falcon

Winter

The hand-saw's fixed and gleaming grin
bit into bark and still-moist cambium,
slowed in the tight-curled pages of a life
as long as his, while yellow dust
peppered the frost-rutted ground
that rebuffed his spade, that held him off
from work more surely than a shaken head.

The baulks of timber, stacked against
a hard time such as this, shortened
slowly through a finger-numbing hour,
and then the sawn logs in their sack burned
into his bent back all up the hill
and through woods silenced by the cold
dust of December on every surface.

Bethlehem seemed very far away.
Stopping half up the climb out of the ghyll,
sack down, head back, mouth wide for breath,
in silence and slow motion a sparrowhawk flew
into the line between his eyes and, high up,
the falcon. His omen. For good: sometimes for ill.
Not much to go on, but something...

Spring

He came down Blue Hill at five
with dirty hands, cracked nails,
paint from some rainy day's work
still in clefts and creases;
shrugging the bait-bag strap
back on his shoulder, touching
a thin fold of notes curled
round his buttock, a small weight
of coins proclaiming each step.
With something at last to show
he'd get a bottle, her favourite,
to drown that morning's hard words
and tears; a bottle to make her
tipsy and wanton, and so to bed.
Anticipation bunched in his groin.
Then on the pavement their friend
Kate frozen in horror, hands pressed
to cheeks, staring at him, his smile,
his wave, his incomprehension:

You don't know yet, do you? Do you?
Oh God oh Christ oh God oh God oh

Omen

Before the tilting fells could spill
the falcon from their folds she soared
up out of shadow into silver
and blue, and above the rim, silvered,

spun earth beneath her, casually.
The shining air obeyed her wings.
Below, the long gulf of valley
still deep with green shadow, emptying,

in which a whorl of blackness squirmed.
In a thousand feet of fall the falcon's
pinions shrieked and hummed,
scattering a nervous gang of ravens

from the huge table of stone
and the spreadeagled man
and his screaming mouth open
and his eyes hooked into her own.

The Stone Golgotha

I

Amber
leaks from cupped fells
ultramarine
from sky's broad gulf

curlews
bubble, a single raven
croaks.

A drum!
Snipe drumming steep air
blood
beating in time

having
cast off from grief
into pain

flesh maps rock
every crevice and knot
welcoming agony
with outstretched arms

spread legs
buttocks scourged by
stone knuckles

dreaming
her fingers soothed
fetches
raw stinging tears

waking
to clouds weeping
salt rain.

II

Voices

midmorning, clouds
clearing fetch
walkers to the track
hidden below

a woman's laughter

not like hers

that last morning
hard words and tears.
Why can't you, why
can't you understand?

The twins feeding
owl-eyed, afraid.
Turn away, leave
bright the doorway

hard sun burning

flesh and eyes

stare in reproach.

Late afternoon
a single small cloud
writhes and boils
an infant demon

black-bellied, drops

warm drops on dry
distended tongue
swallow, drink down
the hot brief storm

ah, but why?

Set face against
judas survival
let the rain hiss
on thirsty stone

dusk brings a wind
to chill this
useless and aching
piss-wet groin.

III

Their bodies lie in the cold
radius of my spread limbs

their untouched faces   three
full white moons betrayed

by weak flesh   the quick exit
of breath   of breath   of breath

breathe shallow chest
release your intolerable hold

on life that sets me apart
from these I did not love

enough

I sink down   they rise   dead
eyes burning   torches   stars

arc-lights illuminate my guilt
I cannot hide   the stone clasps

my flesh

writhes   arching ankle to wrist
uselessly   lie again

outstretched   an insect spiked
on this numb shard of broken world

I wait

nameless and lost for them to come
once more with night-black daggers

for cold heart eye's treachery
the tongue in my scream-wide mouth

Return

After the ravens had gone
he lifted his head from the stone
better to follow the falcon. His name
returned to him... and then he saw
that bird's cross mock his own.
Silvered in streams of light
the falcon soared again and turned
down-valley, slowly transformed
from crucifix to line by flight.

As though limbs learned
for the first time to move,
as though life for the first time
engaged his attention, he climbed
down from his stone, bearing
indentures of rock in his flesh,
and followed the miner's track
through woods and small fields
to the last green crest

and stood with the sun on his back
and his long shadow reaching down
and his arms outstretched.